THE BOOK OF THE HAMBURGS

LECTOR HOUSE PUBLIC DOMAIN WORKS

THE BOOK OF THE HAMBURGS

LYMAN FRANK BAUM

ISBN: 978-93-5420-988-8

Published: 1886

LECTOR HOUSE LLP
E-MAIL: lectorpublishing@gmail.com

THE BOOK OF THE HAMBURGS

A BRIEF TREATISE UPON THE MATING, REARING AND MANAGEMENT OF THE DIFFERENT VARIETIES OF HAMBURGS.

BY

L. FRANK BAUM

1886

CONTENTS

Page

- THE BOOK OF THE HAMBURGS. 1
  - » EARLY HISTORY. 1
  - » CHARACTERISTICS OF HAMBURGS. 2
  - » BLACK HAMBURGS. 5
  - » THE SILVER-SPANGLED HAMBURG. 12
  - » GOLDEN-SPANGLED HAMBURGS. 15
  - » SILVER-PENCILED HAMBURGS. 18
  - » GOLDEN-PENCILED HAMBURGS. 23
  - » WHITE HAMBURGS. 25
  - » CARE OF YOUNG CHICKS. 27
  - » PREPARING HAMBURGS FOR EXHIBITION. 28
  - » HINTS TO JUDGES. 30

THE BOOK OF THE HAMBURGS.

Long before what we now call "fancy fowls" were known or recognized (in fact, long before the memory of any person now living), Hamburgs were kept and bred to feather among the peasants of Yorkshire and Lancashire in England, and by them exhibited at the small town and county fairs in their neighborhood. Of course they were then known under different names, the Blacks being called "Black Pheasant Fowls" and the Spangled varieties "Lancashire Mooneys" and "Yorkshire Pheasants"; while such a variety as the Penciled Hamburgs were either wholly unknown or else were so little thought of that they have left no record of their origin, if, indeed, they are natives of England at all.

EARLY HISTORY.

Mr. Wright, who has traced these fowls back still further, inclines to the belief that at some period whereof we have no knowledge the Penciled varieties formed a part of the Hamburg family, although our earliest positive knowledge traces them to direct importations from Holland, where they were brought in great numbers, and were originally known under the names of "Dutch Everyday Layers" or "Dutch Everlasting Layers."

As such a thing as a black or spangled variety of this fowl was utterly unknown in Holland, it is presumable that at some period the penciled varieties were exported to Holland and there bred and cherished, while they were allowed to run out or sink into insignificance in England. We cling to this belief so tenaciously on account of the wonderful similitude which marks the characteristics of the Hamburg family, in spite of the fact that one branch came from Holland and the other is emphatically English. These two branches, namely, the Penciled and the Spangles and Blacks, resemble no other varieties of fowls in the slightest degree, while their common characteristics are the absence of the incubating instinct, clean, slender legs, neat rose combs, small, round and white ear-lobes, and the light, but sweeping and graceful, lines of form which are wholly their own and unapproachable by any other breed of fowls, no matter how fine their symmetry. If this were not enough to stamp them with certainty of having one origin, we mark the fact that spangled chickens are frequently *penciled* in their first feathers; while, as they mature, the black spangles or moons are often surmounted by a light tip beyond them, thus again approaching the penciled character, while conversely it will be found that if penciled birds be bred too dark the last bar has a strong tendency to become *too wide*, thus approaching a *spangled* character.

If we consider the utter want of interest with which poultry was regarded in the earlier days, and the fact that no traditions of any account relating to fowls have been handed down, we may be justified in believing that these facts prove our conjectures in regard to the original identity of these varieties to be correct. From whence their common progenitor came, we can have no idea, but that they did have one we strongly believe. It may have been that they came from the Blacks, as that variety is thought to be the oldest, and a cross might have resulted in the broken color, or possibly these Blacks having a number of white feathers may have been bred together until a distinctly-marked plumage had been obtained.

Bearing in mind, however, that Aldrovandus speaks of a fowl which strongly resembles the penciled variety as *Gallina Turcica*, it is possible that the Penciled was the original variety, and, as the name suggests, of Eastern origin.

These conjectures and hypotheses are perplexing and unsatisfactory, and are really of no practical value, being only of use in affording another instance of the fascinating problems which constantly present themselves to the poultry fancier of a philosophical and inquiring turn of mind. This much appears to be certain: that of all our many varieties of fancy fowls the Hamburg is by odds the oldest; indeed, Mr. Wingfield claims that old records show that fowls with all the Hamburg characteristics were bred in the yards of monasteries as early as the fourteenth century.

At the great Birmingham show the authorities there, recognizing the general resemblance between the Penciled, Spangled and Black varieties, and the inconvenience of their numerous and varied appellations, grouped them together under the general name of HAMBURGS, by which they have been known since, fanciers accepting with alacrity a name which was at once convenient in classing the breeds and which brought the separated members of what was no doubt a distinct family together, as it is most certain they belong and should be arranged.

Many breeders who have no knowledge of the deliberations at Birmingham have been puzzled to guess why the name Hamburg should have been chosen to designate a family which was mainly English, but these "fathers of the fraternity" had too much business to transact to allow them to inquire very carefully into the early history of this fowl. The Rev. E. S. Dixon proposed "that as the penciled varieties were then imported by the Levant merchants from the port of Hamburg they should all take the general name of Hamburgs," and, indeed, this term is as euphonious and convenient as any other could be.

CHARACTERISTICS OF HAMBURGS.

In usefulness and beauty the Hamburgs stand very prominently amongst that numerous collection of fowls which our broad nomenclature denominates "fancy poultry." The plumage of every variety, either Penciled or Spangled, Silver, Golden or Black, is at once beautiful and striking, attracting the attention of strangers to the poultry yard or exhibition room when all other breeds have failed to interest them, and drawing from them involuntary tributes of admiration. And if they are so much admired by cold and superficial observers, surely the Hamburg fancier may be pardoned for his unbounded enthusiasm for his favorites when every season and nearly every day unfolds new beauties in his birds and renders them more fascinating and delightful to his eye. The exquisite symmetry, the novel and shapely rose combs, the snowy and delicate ear-lobes, the tapering blue legs and graceful carriage give them an aristocratic and "dressed up" appearance and render them the most beautiful of our domestic fowls.

The Hamburg fancier has plenty of scope in which to indulge his taste, the different colors and markings affording an ample variety from which to choose, while the general characteristics are the same.

"Hamburgs," says Mr. Beldon in Lewis Wright's poultry book, "are without doubt the most beautiful breed of poultry we possess, as well as the most useful, all varieties being alike elegant and beautiful. The dweller in the country will generally prefer the Silver, while the citizen will take the Golden or Black; but all of them, in their matchless variety of marking and color, will delight the eye with the utmost degree which is perhaps possible of beauty in fowls. Their marvelous beauty, however, would not recommend the Hamburgs to the practical breeder so much as their wonderful egg-producing qualities, which it has been claimed surpass those of any other breed. The wonderful stories told of Hamburg productiveness, while often more amusing than reliable, serve to show that in any hands, in any climate and under the most adverse circumstances they have proved very profitable to their owners, while with ordinary care they are the best of layers."

The average Hamburg pullet will begin laying at four or five months of age, and will lay from 150 to 200 eggs the first year under favorable circumstances. The second and third years hens will average from 175 to 225 eggs when properly cared for, and from the third year their productiveness gradually declines, although one reliable breeder asserts that he once owned a Black Hamburg hen which at five years of age laid 220 eggs in ten months. A great deal depends upon the strain of birds and the care they receive, as if productive traits are cherished and carefully bred for, the number of eggs may be greatly increased, while neglect to properly cultivate this quality by careless and incompetent breeders will result in a marked decrease in productiveness.

The absence of the incubating instinct has much to do with the productiveness for which Hamburgs are noted, as no time is lost in sitting or brooding the chicks. Some breeders claim that Hamburgs *never* attempt to sit. This is incorrect. We have known cases, although we acknowledge they are rare, where Hamburg hens have hatched and reared goodly broods of chickens, in every case proving themselves steady sitters and excellent mothers; nor was there a particle of tainted blood in their veins, these being merely cases where that wonderful instinct which is common to nearly all fowls will "crop out" occasionally in *every* variety of non-sitting fowls. It is *not* necessarily due to a former cross, but may be occasioned by "reversion" to which we attribute everything that we do not understand in nature's domain.

This non-sitting instinct is of double value to the Hamburgs, as they do not lose half their feathers during incubation, but maintain their sleek appearance through the entire season, and when they do moult they moult easily and rapidly, seldom or never being left for a time denuded of feathers, as are most other breeds, but the new feathers making their appearance as the old ones drop out, so that they are never an eyesore to their owners. Indeed, they seem to change their coats so easily that it is no rare thing for hens to lay as steadily during this ordinarily trying process as at any other time. They should, however, have an extra allowance of feed at this time, and a little tincture of iron in their drinking water or a few rusty nails placed in the drinking pans will strengthen and tone up their systems.

To do their best, Hamburgs should have free range. Mr. Beldon, though greatly overdrawing their need for this luxury, attaches so much importance to it that he says: "They are of little use penned up, in which state they pine and mope for liberty; that bright cheerfulness which is common to them disappears, and from being the happiest they become the most wretched of birds."

Though Mr. Beldon may have found this the case, our own experience has been that no small breeds of fowls will stand the tedium of a long and severe winter in close quarters better than the Hamburgs. In fact, all you need is to *keep them busy*, and they will seem happy and contented. Still, the larger the grass run they have in summer the greater their productiveness and the better they will do. They are very small eaters, and when at liberty are excellent foragers, being up at break of day and away rummaging the fields and pastures in search of food. Their quick eye at once espies their prey, and "woe to the poor worm that happens on that particular morning to have got up a little too early." Every corner is searched with indefatigable zeal, and by the time the man gets around in the morning to feed them they have made a good breakfast and are ready for the business of the day. Perfect liberty or a large grass run are valuable adjuncts to health and egg production. Give it them if you possibly can.

As a rule Hamburgs are a healthy breed, being little subject to the common ailments of poultry. One of our correspondents writes: "They are remarkably hardy, often enduring hardships that to other breeds mean disease and death with successful fortitude. I have had young Hamburg chicks pecked by the mother of a rival flock and virtually 'scalped' in her insane jealousy, the skin being torn from the head down the entire back, and yet the youngster would trot around as lively as though nothing had happened, and not only get well but flourish. Sometimes the feathers would grow out upon the 'skinned' place, and sometimes it would always retain a smooth appearance. I have now a hen, which we consider one of our best breeders, without a vestige of feathering upon her entire back, owing to a like accident in her youth. The chicks are very easily reared. Of course they must have proper care, as they cannot rear themselves; but with a moderate degree of attention no trouble will be found in raising them to maturity.

"Taken as a whole we consider the Hamburgs as hardly excelled by any other fowl for the farmer, fancier or poulterer. On a good homestead they will keep themselves, and if well attended to will pay better than any other farm stock in proportion to the investment. In fine, I feel perfectly safe in an assertion that in no one breed will be found so much beauty and usefulness, and so many excellent qualities, as in the several varieties of the Hamburg family, while in the one item of egg production they stand to-day where they did hundreds of years ago, unrivaled by any domestic fowl."

This is a statement of one who is full of enthusiasm, but it may be noted that only a superior breed of fowls would excite so much commendation in a breeder who has been familiar with them from his youth.

BLACK HAMBURGS.

BLACK HAMBURGS.

Although there is no certainty that this is the oldest variety of fowls, still, as it has a pedigree of nearly 200 years, it is presumable that it was the oldest variety of the Hamburg family. Mr. Beldon considers the claims of the Spangles and Blacks to be about equal as regards age, and rather favors the former. However, a passage in an old book published in London in 1702 by Thomas Sutlief, entitled "A trip to the North of England," has induced us to believe that the Blacks were the oldest breed. It says: "One of my pleasant reminiscences of this county (Lancaster) is the pleasure with which I regarded their pretty fowl, the Black Pheasants, as they call them, and which furnished me many a delicious fresh egg for my breakfast.... The stout peasants regard them with much favor, and point with pride to their white ears and flat combs."

It would seem from this that not only were they the favorite fowls, but that they then possessed in a great measure their present characteristics. If the spangled birds were then known they surely could not have fallen under the observation of this writer, who would have been sure to have noted them from their striking appearance.

Be that as it may, Black Hamburgs are known to have been bred in Lancashire long before the poultry-showing era, and were called by the peasants Black Pheasants. They had the rose comb, but it was much larger than in our present birds, and not nearly so well formed. They also had the white ear-lobe, despite the claims of many breeders that this desirable point came from a cross with the Spanish. There is no doubt that many Blacks have Spanish blood in them, and some prominent English breeders openly acknowledge its existence in their strains. But we have birds to-day that have never known a particle of Spanish blood in their composition, which possess superior qualities over those with the Spanish cross, and which have the white ear-lobe in all its beauty and perfection.

In a recent letter Mr. Beldon says: "The Black Hamburgs I remember perfectly well when I first began the poultry fancy some twenty-seven years ago, but they were not commonly bred at that time. They were a large bird, with rather coarse combs. Since then the Spanish cross has been used to produce them; in fact, I have known them to be bred from a Black Spanish and Spangled Hamburg, and by careful selection brought to much perfection, with better black plumage, bright red faces and pure white ear-lobes."

Black Pheasants did not formerly possess the exquisite symmetry which is so marked in our present birds, being coarse and short-legged, while the most attention was paid to that resplendent greenish sheen which forms their chief attraction and renders them to-day the most beautiful of black fowls.

There have been many and clever expedients devised to show that the Black Hamburgs came from crossing. Mr. Seebay says: "I have been told by reliable persons that Black Pheasants have been shown for prizes, such as copper kettles, etc., more than a hundred years before my time. The true Silver-Spangled is almost black in one stage of its chicken plumage, and as I have known them produce chickens almost black, and as the shape of the Spangles and Blacks is exactly the same, I had always thought one sprung from the other." This theory is the most plausible one we know of, and is also endorsed by Mr. Sergeantson. The most absurd assertion is that they are the result of a cross between the Golden-Spangled Hamburgs and the Spanish, which is easily refuted by our positive knowledge of their great age. There is no doubt but that some Black Hamburgs (so-called) have been made from this cross, as Mr. Beldon says; but the unfortunate breeder who gets any of these fowls into his yards, will soon discover from a plentiful sprinkling of single combs in his chicks and a general want of fixed characteristics, that he has been imposed upon. It is not of great importance to know exactly how they did originate, as from a practical point of view it is enough to know that they are now a firmly established breed of great beauty and undoubted excellence.

The Black Hamburgs lay the largest eggs of any variety of this breed, while in numbers they fully equal the Spangled and Penciled. They are therefore much sought after by those who wish to obtain eggs for the market as well as for the table, and are perhaps the most popular variety of Hamburgs.

Plumage.—This is the most important point in the Black Hamburg, though it has been much neglected by American breeders. It should be exceedingly soft, the feathers having a feeling as of satin to the hand, and a deep but distinct and beautiful gloss or tinge. Much weight should be given to this in both sexes, although it can be cultivated to a greater extent in the female than in the male. This green gloss should not appear on the end of the feathers only, but throughout the entire plumage—*the greener and richer the color the better*. To be seen to advantage this beautiful gloss should be viewed in a strong light or when the sun is upon the bird. You then see that sheen in which they surpass all other black fowls. The color required is the green black; the purple, bluish or raven black so often seen is very undesirable, and should be avoided. These colors are so distinct that there is no liability to mistake the true shade. Some strains are of a deep blue green, almost a steel blue; these have green tails. Other strains are of a lighter green; these have bronze green tails. The purer the green and the less admixture of any other tinge the better. Never breed from birds which seem to be penciled with bluish purple. It is often caused by a late and protracted moult, and may appear in birds which as chicks had the green tinge in all its perfection; but more often it is hereditary. Lancashire fanciers called this mazarine, and it appeared principally on backs of hens or flights of cocks. As we have mentioned, this glossy tinge is not so uniform on the male as the female birds, and this is seemingly in direct opposition to the usual decrees of Nature, which seems to have ordained that the male part of creation be more brilliant than the opposite gender. We are pleased to observe, however, a marked improvement in the plumage of cocks of late years, and hope to see the time when the male bird will show this characteristic as fully as the female.

In Black Hamburg cocks the breast, back, shoulders and tail should be a rich green, the wing-coverts exceedingly brilliant and the outer web of the secondaries (*i. e.,* the whole of the lower part of the closed wing) almost as bright; the lesser tail-coverts are also very rich in color.

Tegetmeier speaks of *spangling* being visible in Black Hamburgs when seen in the sunlight. The birds he examined must have been decidedly poor ones, or perhaps it was his misfortune to see those birds *compounded* of Golden-Spangled Hamburgs and Spanish which we have spoken of. Such cross-bred birds will show the iridescent green spangle Mr. Tegetmeier has spoken of, but which we have never been able to discern on good birds of a pure strain.

Occasionally rich red or orange colored feathers will crop out in Black Hamburg cockerels—very seldom in pullets. These red feathers come from what we suppose was pheasant blood at some remote period introduced into these birds, or perhaps a part of their original make-up, and do not by any means prove the existence of impure blood. It is the result of our strenuous efforts to keep up and improve the greenish luster, and invariably comes from highly colored birds. These birds are sometimes of great use to breeders, and enable us to obtain finely colored birds by mating them with dead-black pullets.

BLACK HAMBURGS.

But while we may tolerate an occasional showing of red feathers (which only appear in the hackle, as in the Golden Pheasant), we must be very severe on birds showing those of another color—namely, *white* feathers. There seems to be a natural tendency to show the white feathers in all black fowls, and this evil has been so stubborn to eradicate that Mr. Felch, at a meeting of the American Poultry Association, offered a resolution to allow white tips to appear in exhibition birds. The many evils which would thus arise from lowering our ideal *Standard* for this magnificent variety were so obvious that the members of that Association promptly rejected the resolution at a later meeting in Cleveland, Ohio. We know not whether most to blame the futile efforts of Mr. Felch to accommodate the variety to the wants of a few incompetent breeders, or to applaud the wisdom of our brethren of the A. P. A. in "squelching" such innovations. They surely have the thanks of all honest breeders of Black Hamburgs, which can be bred *black* as well as any other variety of black fowls, if we only have patience and honestly strive to eradicate this serious fault, which, if allowed, would work to the disadvantage of all.

Comb.—There is no style of comb so difficult to breed to perfection as the rose comb, and the excellent combs shown on Black and Spangled Hamburgs at our recent shows prove how much can be accomplished by judicious breeding. To our eye it is beautiful and elegant, and forms one of the chief attractions of the Hamburg. It should be a deep, rich red; not so large as to overhang the eyes or beak; square in front; fitting close and straight on the head; not inclining to one side; not hollow in the center—on the contrary, we prefer a slight rise in the center, although an even comb throughout is better. It should be uniform on each side; the top covered with small points, and terminating in a spike behind, which inclines upward very slightly. The absence of this spike is a grave defect, which if a natural blemish disqualifies a bird by the *American Standard of Excellence*, as does likewise a comb so large as to obstruct the sight.

Ear-Lobes.—The ear-lobe is one of the most striking features of the Black Hamburg, and in connection with the bright red comb and greenish plumage, form a *tout ensemble* such as no one can see without admiring. The ear-lobe on the old Black Hamburgs was smaller than it is nowadays, although it is noticeable that those birds which have been kept pure have a smaller and finer ear-lobe than those which were crossed with the Spanish. As we have before observed, Mr. Beldon (in common with some other breeders, who all ought to know better) has thought that the white ear-lobe was only introduced by the Spanish cross, an error which we have furnished abundant evidence to refute; so that really all that was gained by this unnecessary cross was a large, pendent ear-lobe, which is totally at variance with our accepted ideas as to what a Hamburg ear-lobe should be. It has been allowed by most judges, until quite recently, to be a little larger in the Blacks than in any other variety of Hamburgs, but it must be pure white, well rounded, lying smoothly and close to the face, like a piece of white kid glove, and *the smaller the better*. A large, pendent ear-lobe, like that of the Spanish and Leghorns, is certainly a grave blemish; nor should it be wrinkled or puffy, or at all tinged with red about the edges.

The Face.—One of our chief difficulties in breeding Hamburgs is the tendency to white in the face, which should be a deep, rich crimson, almost scarlet. A white face is a positive disqualification, and a dark gypsy face much to be avoided. Both these latter defects owe their origin to the Spanish cross, although white specks in the face will often appear in pure-bred birds as they advance in age. By careful breeding, and judiciously selecting those cocks which retain a pure red face, this may be entirely bred out, while breeding from birds showing the white face fixes the defect in the progeny, and causes much trouble to the breeder before it can be eradicated. It is rare to find a two or three-year-old cock which does not show a patch of white under the eye or near the ear-lobe; but the graver and more common the fault, the more pains should be taken to breed it out, and we have no doubt but the time will soon come when such a thing as a white-specked face in the show room will be unknown. We trust efforts will be made in this direction.

Legs and Tail.—The legs should be a *dark*, leaden blue, approaching black, in young birds, as the tendency is to grow light with age. Light blue legs in a cockerel or pullet are very objectionable.

The tail in male birds should be long, well curved, and graceful, flowing rather backward from the rump. A squirrel tail is a grave fault—a disqualification, in fact—as is also a wry tail or one carried constantly to one side. Wry tails have various causes, originating sometimes from accident, but they are often hereditary, and wry-tailed birds should never be used for breeding. Often the cramped quarters of an exhibition coop will render a bird temporarily wry-tailed, or rather induce it for a time to carry it to one side. This will usually disappear when the bird is given full range, but is quite an unfortunate circumstance, as a prize bird is often thrown out on this account.

Symmetry.—This means a great deal in Hamburgs; and as no breed is more symmetrical or graceful in form, particular pains should be taken to prevent them from running into a Game or Dorking shape. We have often seen breeders send birds to the show room which were good in all other points, but most degenerate in symmetry. We heard a prominent judge say lately that "symmetry could not be expressed; it was something about which every man had his own ideas, and applied to birds according to his judgment." Each breed has its distinct symmetry of proportions, and it would be no more absurd to expect a Cochin shape on a Hamburg than it is to admit a Hamburg to be well proportioned with the slender neck, long legs, and high station of a Game, or the heavy, square and dumpy appearance of the Dorking. In fact they must be *real Hamburgs* in shape; neck medium length, and carried well over the back; back not very long or very short; breast full, prominent and wide; wings good size, the points carried comparatively low; tail ample and well spread out, and carried rather erect; thighs well rounded and of medium length; shanks slender, smooth and neat; carriage showing gracefulness and activity. By no means must they carry the idea of being Black Dorkings, or Rose-combed Spanish, or worse yet, untrimmed Games. Avoid also narrow bodies and whip tails.

Points in Breeding Black Hamburgs.—In mating any variety for breeding, the faults to which they are most liable should be borne in mind, and the breeder's one idea be to breed them out, and so perfect the birds as much as possible. This in some instances may take years of careful and painstaking matings; years of disappointment and chagrin may follow, as we see the defects still cropping out, and realize the failure of all our carefully-laid plans. But how glorious is the feeling enjoyed by the fancier when at last skill triumphs, and he beholds in a numerous and nearly perfected progeny the result of years of toil and study. Then it is that he hies him joyfully to the show room; then it is that he triumphs over the breeder who has so long plucked the premiums from under his nose; and as he returns home, after enjoying his first genuine success, his thoughts are employed as to the best means of further improving his birds; and to such men—studious, painstaking and persevering—we owe that perfection in our domestic fowls which is so astonishing, considering the short time that has been devoted to their improvement, and which ought to convince us how pliable and plastic fancy poultry is in the hands of an intelligent breeder. Do not be discouraged by failure at first—*keep trying*, and the time must and will come when your efforts shall be crowned with success.

Black Hamburgs are not a very difficult fowl to breed, when you go about it understandingly. In selecting breeding stock, we again say, bear in mind the defects to which they are heir—namely, badly-shaped combs, white faces, pendent and over-sized ear-lobes, legginess, and white or red feathers.

At shows color in cocks is not regarded so much as it is in pullets—not nearly so much as it ought to be. "Although," says Mr. Sergeantson, "other things being equal, color will carry the day." Therefore for breeding cockerels, choose the best combed birds; good, red faces, free from white; round, small ear-lobes; free from red or colored feathers in any part of the plumage, and short legs, broad breast and back. Squirrel tails result quite often from narrow-bodied birds, and this, besides being very objectionable, is hereditary, so bear this last requisite well in mind. We have said nothing about color in this mating, for the reason that it is not considered of so much consequence in cockerels as in pullets; but if, with the above requisites, you can find a *male* bird with good color, you may breed in the progeny this very desirable quality.

Now for pullet breeding (if you are able to have two pens; if not, choose the above mating), it is absolutely requisite that in addition to the above qualifications, or as many of them as can be obtained, a *cock* be found which has a brilliant luster to his plumage. As we have intimated, it is very difficult to find a cock with this brilliant plumage without a touch of red in hackle. If you *can* obtain him, well and good; if not, bear in mind the red feathers, but use him, for color in cock you *must* have above any other consideration for breeding pullets. The Rev. Mr. Sergeantson, whom we have before quoted, and who had greater success than any other English breeder with this variety, entirely agrees with us in this. He says: "I would much rather choose for the purpose a red-hackled cock, if good in other respects, than a dull-colored one. I have often bred beautiful, lustrous pullets from hens with very little color, when mated with a bright cock; but never from a dull-colored cock, however lustrous the hens with him might be." Moreover, in this pen, choose birds with small or moderately sized combs, as there is a general tendency in combs of pullets to lop over, if bred too large.

Do not be discouraged, if you cannot obtain all these points at once; get as near to it as possible; and every succeeding year will find you drawing nearer and nearer to that desired goal—*perfection*.

SILVER-SPANGLED HAMBURGS.

THE SILVER-SPANGLED HAMBURG.

This variety is probably as well known and generally bred as any variety of fancy poultry we have, and its continued popularity is conclusive proof of the high estimation in which it is held by fanciers throughout the land. To the counties of Lancashire and Yorkshire the Silver-Spangled Hamburgs owe their present state of perfection, although American breeders have done more in twenty years to perfect their combs, ear-lobes and face than English fanciers have been able to accomplish in twice that time. The plumage is essentially English, and to English fanciers is due the credit for perfecting their beautiful markings. In fact, they were brought to a high standard of excellence in Lancashire long before the first poultry show; and this standard was clearly defined and adhered to by fanciers, who were chary about admitting innovations as to their ideas.

They were originally called Silver Pheasants in Yorkshire, and Silver Mooneys in Lancashire. These latter, while the most numerous and best bred, admitted only hen-feathered cocks, and were brought to a high state of perfection. Mr. Beldon says: "Some of the old Mooneys were absolute perfection in point of feather; the spangling, so large, round and rich in color, was really something to be wondered at, and shows a skill and enthusiasm in breeding which, in the absence of public shows in those days, has about it something of the marvelous."

When poultry shows first came into fashion these Mooneys received the lion's share of the awards at all the exhibitions, until it came to be considered utter foolishness to pit any kind of fowl against them, and they enjoyed their exalted position for several years unmolested. At the expiration of this time, however, breeders of the Mooneys were thrown into confusion by the sudden and unanimous decree of the judges that these "hen-feathered Mooneys" were all humbug, and not "the correct thing," inasmuch as so many of these "hen-feathered" cocks proved unprolific or imperfect that long-tailed birds were secretly used to keep up the breed. There was so much evident truth in this that the struggle, though sharp, was of short duration; the judges triumphed, and the reign of the Silver Mooneys as show birds was over, while the star of the Silver Pheasants steadily rose, until nothing was recognized but the full-plumaged cocks, though the hens still lacked the nice spangling which had rendered the Lancashire birds so much admired, the spangles being small and indistinct. It may be well to state here that the Yorkshire birds were the original variety, the excellence in spangling attained by the Lancashire fanciers being the result of judicious breeding. The Yorkshire birds had better symmetry, whiter ear-lobes, smaller combs and clearer tails, and it is from them that our modern Silver-Spangled Hamburgs are descended. They are fully up to the other varieties in productiveness, and possess all the good traits of the breed, while their exceeding beauty renders them remarkably attractive.

Plumage.—Of course the spangling in the Silver-Spangled Hamburg is of primary importance, and should be regarded with the utmost care. As the spangling differs in the sexes, we shall be obliged to describe them separately.

Cock.—The neck-hackle should be abundant, descending well over the shoulders, and in color, silvery-white (any approach to a yellowish tinge to be carefully avoided), the longer feathers ending in a small diamond-shaped spangle, and presenting a beautiful rayed appearance about the shoulders.

The back and saddle should have the same general style of feathers, pure white in color, except the small spangle near the end as in the neck-hackle, avoiding any appearance of the yellowish tinge.

The breast feathers should be pure silvery-white, each feather ending with a well-defined, round, large-sized greenish-black spangle or moon, showing as little white on the tip as possible, the spangles increasing in size in proportion as the feather increases in size. The body and wing-feathers must have a similar moon-shaped spangle. There is a tendency to indistinct or smutty markings in the tail, which should be avoided. The moons on the breast-feathers should be just large enough to give the breast a spangled appearance, by allowing a little of the white beyond each moon to show. The moons, if too large, give the breast a mossed or black appearance, which is a defect. The spangles on greater and lesser wing-coverts form two distinct bars across the wing, which is very requisite in a well-marked bird. Care should be taken to avoid clear white feathers in back and saddle, as they are very liable to appear in light-colored birds.

Hen.—The neck-hackle should be composed of clear, silvery-white feathers, each plainly striped near the end with greenish-black. The back, breast and body should be clear white, each feather distinctly spangled with a large, round and greenish-black moon, as large as possible without the spangles running together and giving a mossy or black appearance in places.

The half-moon spangle should be avoided with much care in all feathers except the wing-secondaries, where it is allowable in both sexes. The wing-coverts, greater or lesser, should be clear, silvery-white, terminating in a large, greenish-black, round spangle, and forming two parallel bars, distinctly marked, across the wing. It is difficult to find a perfectly spangled tail without some black or smutty color in the main body of the feathers; this is not so persistent a defect in the hen as in the cock, and can be bred out of both, if proper care is taken. The feathers on the thighs should be as distinct as possible, care being taken to prevent a mossy or laced appearance.

Nothing can be more beautiful than a finely-spangled Silver Hamburg, and when a perfect spangling is once attained, it is easily continued in the progeny. Laced or half-moon feathers are a great eye-sore to the fancier, and are often very troublesome, although perhaps not more so than the indistinct markings on the tail, once so common, but which is now being replaced by clear, well-spangled tails—another evidence of skillful breeding.

Other Points.—The comb in Silver-Spangled Hamburgs should resemble exactly that described in our section on Black Hamburgs. The ear-lobe should also be the same, but is more easily bred to perfection in the Spangled than in the Black variety, being naturally rather smaller and smoother; but, on the other hand, more liable to red edges. There is the same tendency to white in the face in Silver-Spangled as in Black Hamburgs, although in a lesser degree, and there surely is no excuse for its cropping out here, if ordinary care is taken to prevent it.

The carriage of Silver-Spangled Hamburgs is graceful in the extreme and constitutes one of their chief attractions; indeed, we think they are among the most stylish birds we have. The legs should be slender, neat and clean, of medium length, and in color, blue or slaty-blue. We have already described what constitutes good symmetry in a Hamburg; let it suffice to say that the Silver-Spangled are essentially *Hamburg* in this respect.

The disqualifications to which this variety is liable are absence of the wing-bars, markings wholly crescent-shaped or of the half-moon character, solid black breasts, laced feathers, squirrel tails, red ear-lobes, and the absence of spike in comb, cocks hen-feathered.

The beak should be horn-color, and the eyes a dark hazel. Care should be taken to avoid a black fluff in either sex, as it is an especial abomination to the intelligent fancier.

Points in Breeding Silver-Spangled Hamburgs. — We are obliged to acknowledge that unless you have a thorough knowledge of the strain you are breeding from, there is considerable guess-work necessary in choosing a Silver-Spangled Hamburg cock for breeding; for the reason that, unlike most fowls, there are frequent cases where a finely-marked cock will fail to throw a good percentage of well-marked chicks in his progeny. So, if you fail to procure a good breeder at first, you must try again. In the first place, select a cock with good comb and ear-lobes, as much spangling in back and saddle as possible, good wing-bars, and clear tail; in fact, a good, deep-colored show cock, and put him to the very best hens you can get.

Care must be taken to avoid any grave faults on either side, such as smudgy markings, poor ear-lobes, or overhanging, coarse combs. Now see what you can do with this mating. If you get a fair proportion of well-marked chicks, stick to this pen as long as they will breed, or the eggs are fertile, for it is not every lot that breeds well together. If you find that you are not getting a good proportion of fairly-marked birds, you must change the cock, procuring one from another strain, and try your luck with him, persevering until you get what you desire. In all varieties of fowls there are some strains that will produce better cockerels than pullets, and *vice versa*, and Hamburgs are no exception to the general rule. You may, therefore, find it to your advantage to breed from two different yards, provided you have sufficient room and the means of procuring the proper birds. If a pen breeds excellent cockerels but poor pullets, keep that pen for cockerel breeding, as it is far better to breed good birds of one sex than middling birds of both sexes, even if you have but one pen. When you have a good pen of cockerel getters, begin to look about for a yard which will breed fine pullets. A little patience and perseverance will be amply repaid when at last you find yourself successful; and when you *do* get what you want, stick to it!

Our instructions for mating Silver-Spangled Hamburgs are *in toto* as minute as ever have or can be given, for the simple reason, as we have said, that your first matings (unless you know the strain well) must be greatly influenced by chance.

We might add that whenever you select a cock for breeding, choose one of as much health and vigor as you can find possessing the other requisite points, for we believe that nothing contributes more to distinct markings in chickens than parents that can give them vigorous constitutions and hardy characteristics.

GOLDEN-SPANGLED HAMBURGS.

GOLDEN-SPANGLED HAMBURGS.

About thirty years ago, when poultry shows first came into fashion, there were two kinds of Golden-Spangled Hamburgs. One was called the Golden Pheasants, and was a fine, large bird, but as a rule the cocks were hen-feathered. The spangling was very fine, and the groundwork a dull bay, but there was a great deal of smut in all their markings. They were good layers, had white ear-lobes, and moderately good combs. The other variety were called Golden Mooneys, and in color and markings were very superior to the Golden Pheasants. Mr. Beldon, in "Wright's Poultry Book," says: "I shall never forget my feelings of pleasure on first seeing the Golden Mooney hen. She struck me as being something wonderful. The ground color of the plumage in these fowls is of the very richest bay, the spangling very bold and clear, and of a green, satin-looking black; in fact, the plumage was so rich and glossy that the full beauty of it could not be seen, except in the sunshine, but when it *was* seen, it formed a picture never to be forgotten. I am here speaking of the hen; the cock's plumage was also of the very richest description."

The cocks, however, had solid black breasts and their ear-lobes consisted of little more than a bit of red skin, such as we see upon Games. By degrees, as hen-feathered cocks and red ear-lobes came to be considered great blemishes, these two varieties were bred together, and from them is derived our modern Golden-Spangled Hamburgs. They are a little larger than the Silver-Spangled; but, while they lay a trifle larger egg, do not produce quite so many of them. They are very hardy, and exceedingly attractive in appearance, being the richest colored of any variety of the Hamburgs, excepting the Black.

Plumage.—The plumage of the Golden-Spangled Hamburgs differs in many respects from that of the Silver-Spangled. The ground color is a rich, deep golden-bay, and should be as even throughout as possible. There is a tendency to run lighter in color under the breast and body. This is a serious blemish. The neck-hackle, instead of being spangled, as in the Silver variety, has a long black stripe running the entire length of the feather to the extremity of the tip. This stripe should be a glossy, greenish-black, standing out well defined from the ground color, and not clouded. The saddle is composed of similar feathers. Both saddle and hackle should be abundant, the latter flowing well over the shoulders, especially in the cocks—of course the females have no saddles. The breast, back and body feathers should be a rich, golden-bay, each feather ending with a large, distinct, round, black spangle, having a rich greenish luster. The wing primaries and secondaries in the cock are bay on the outer web, and black on the inner web, each feather ending with a black, metallic crescent. On the hen the primaries and secondaries are a clear golden-bay, each feather ending with a black, metallic crescent. The wing-bows should be a clear, deep golden-bay, each feather tipped with a large, round, greenish-black spangle; the greater and lesser wing-coverts a clear golden-bay, each feather ending with a large, oblong, greenish-black spangle, forming two distinct bars, parallel across the wing. The tail should be a rich greenish-black in both sexes, full and well expanded. In cocks the sickles are well curved and glossy, and the tail-feathers abundant and of a rich, metallic luster.

One of the most common defects in this variety is feathers tipped beyond the spangle with a small edging of bay or white; sometimes both appear, one beyond the other. Although this is to be avoided, it is not a direct disqualification. We have often seen it appear upon old birds whose plumage was previously entirely innocent of such markings, and it is rare, indeed, to find a pair of old exhibition birds entirely without it, to say nothing of breeding fowls. It makes its appearance chiefly upon the breast and body, but is also frequently seen in the hackle. We hope to see the time when this defect shall be wholly eradicated. The white tips are the most objectionable, but are nearly as common as the bay edgings to the spangles. The entire plumage should be close and glossy, and very rich and uniform in color and markings.

Other Points.—The comb on Golden-Spangled Hamburgs is liable to be coarse and large, although in finely-bred birds we often find as good combs as are ever seen upon the other varieties. A tendency to red edgings in ear-lobes (which should be a pure white) is also to be avoided. In size this variety surpasses the Silver-Spangled Hamburgs, but they lose in symmetry usually what they gain in size, consequently symmetry is a point which should be carefully looked after. There is not much tendency to white face, which is seldom observed in birds of this variety. The legs should be of medium length, shanks clean and slender, and in color leaden-blue. The tail is one of their chief beauties, and should claim much attention from the breeder, care being taken to guard against wry or squirrel tails, which are very liable to descend to the offspring.

Points in mating Golden-Spangled Hamburgs. — We do not know of a single case where any one has given instructions for mating this variety which are at all clear or definite, or offer the slightest assistance to the breeder. Even our distinguished English contemporaries give it up in despair. One of our correspondents writes as follows:

"At a large exhibition several years ago we inquired of a gentleman who had won nearly all the awards on Golden Spangles — and with excellently marked birds, too — what his system or mating was by which he procured such fine birds. With something that resembled a sneer at our remarks, he said: 'I let them breed themselves!' We had then been trying our best for some time to study the characteristics of the breed, in order to obtain some clue by which to mate them properly; and this remark, together with the living proofs of the good results of such indiscriminate matings before our eyes, we must confess rather staggered us. We went home and carefully thought it over, and adhering to our former notions that science would finally triumph, we persevered in our experimental matings, and had the pleasure two years after of defeating the same breeder most thoroughly in the show room. His birds were by this time little more than mongrels — the result of his plan to 'let them breed themselves!'"

In breeding this variety there should be two pens — one to breed males, and one females. In breeding for cockerels, select a large, well-marked cock, whose ground color is a deep, rich golden-bay throughout, free from smutty or cloudy markings, with fine, glossy plumage, the spangles of which possess in a high degree the beautiful metallic, greenish luster. With him mate pullets of medium color (care being taken not to have them too light or dark in the ground color), whose spangles are large and distinct, without running into each other and giving them an undesirable spotted appearance. These pullets should possess good glossy plumage, but size is not requisite, nor need they necessarily have extra-fine combs and ear-lobes, provided the cock possesses these desirable qualities in a marked degree, for it is from him that these qualities are inherited, while the pullet furnishes the color and markings in a greater degree. Especial pains should be taken to choose a cock with a small, fine comb and pure white ear-lobes, when they can be found in connection with the requisite points mentioned.

In breeding for pullets choose a dark-colored cockerel, with good ear-lobes, small comb and good symmetry, and simply mate him with the very best hens you can find. There is a tendency in hens of this variety to become a rather dull, light bay in ground color as they grow aged — these are the very hens to mate with the above-described cockerel. Care should be taken to procure the very best comb, ear-lobes, and symmetry you can find.

With these matings you can hardly fail to breed a good proportion of fine chicks; but, as we have said in connection with the Silver-Spangled Hamburgs, you may not find a cock at first that will prove a good breeder. If not, you must keep on trying. In both the varieties of Spangled Hamburgs the *strain* has a great deal to do in furnishing good breeders. "Blood will tell;" and we should call the attention of the breeder of both these varieties to the necessity of establishing a strain of his own as soon as possible, whose good qualities he will be able to know thoroughly, and whose bad ones he will promptly recognize and endeavor to counterbalance by proper matings.

SILVER-PENCILED HAMBURGS.

SILVER-PENCILED HAMBURGS.

We have already stated that the Penciled Hamburgs were imported into England from Holland, where they first attracted the attention of English fanciers, and although there can be no possible doubt in the mind of an intelligent observer that they originally possessed, with the Spangled and Black varieties, a common progenitor, still they possess several distinctly different characteristics. This is owing, no doubt, to their being so long bred and undoubtedly perfected in a different country and by a different class of people. These differences consist chiefly in a smaller and finer form than the Spangled and Blacks—a smaller head, a smarter appearance, and perhaps more activity, their motions being very quick and graceful. That they are great layers of a small but exquisitely white and finely-flavored egg is proverbial, and on their first introduction into England this quality procured for them the title of "Dutch everlasting layers."

The Silver-Penciled Hamburg is a very beautiful bird, and is greatly admired by every one who can see any beauty at all in a finely-marked and gracefully formed fowl. Indeed, we believe that they have the most *finished* appearance of any fowl, their markings being so fine and regular that there seems nothing more to be desired to entitle them to the palm for beauty.

CREOLES.

This variety, besides the name which we have given, were also called "Chit-tiprats," and still later, "Bolton Grays," under which name they were wide-ly disseminated, and even yet we believe that in some sections they still retain this appellation, although all other names are very rapidly giving way to that of Silver-Penciled Hamburgs. "Creole" was a name also applied to a variety of Sil-ver-Penciled Hamburgs, the markings of the feathers of which were very similar to those of the standard Silver-Penciled Hamburgs (see cut). The "Bolton Grays" were simply Silver-Penciled Hamburgs "run to seed," the pencilings being mossy or smutty.

They are a numerous and attractive class at our poultry exhibitions, and are gaining ground yearly in popular favor; we have even known instances where breeders of Silver-Spangled Hamburgs have discarded them in favor of the Pen-ciled varieties, although we think that the former, in their way, are fully as beau-tiful and desirable.

Silver-Penciled Hamburgs, as chicks, are quite tender, but when fully feathered they are as little liable to disease as any fowl we know of. They are great foragers, and will almost keep themselves, with good range, being happy and contented anywhere and shelling out quantities of eggs under most adverse circumstances.

Plumage.—In the male bird the plumage of the head, hackle, back, saddle, breast and thighs, should be a clear, silvery-white. The yellowish tinge so often seen upon these feathers is a very grave fault, and one that will not be tolerated by a good judge. There is often a tendency to penciled or smutty markings on the under-color of the back—that is, it can only be seen by raising the top feathers. This is also a serious defect, and should be avoided. The tail proper is black, the sickles and tail-coverts being a rich green-black, with a fine and distinct edging of white.

BOLTON GRAYS.

This is the most difficult point to obtain in the plumage of the entire bird in any degree of perfection—indeed, a perfectly-marked tail is seldom seen in a cock. Some birds have marbled tails; others have the sickles splashed with white, which is equally objectionable, as the only white which should be in the tail is the clear edging. The wing appears almost white when closed; but the *inner* webs of the wing-coverts should be darkly penciled. A fine black edging should be observed on the wing-coverts, caused by the ends of the *outer* webs being also slightly tipped with black, which gives the appearance of a slight and indistinct bar on the wing. This point should be distinctly observable, but not too coarse or heavy. The color of the secondary quills is also important. They should be white on the outer web, except a narrow strip of black next the quill, only seen when the wing is opened out, the wing appearing white when closed. The inner web is black, except a narrow white or gray edging. The fluff should be slightly penciled or gray. In the hen the neck-hackle should be pure white, entirely free from any marking whatever. The remainder of the plumage should be a clear, silvery-white, each feather distinctly penciled or marked across with bars of black, as clear and distinct as possible and in particular *as straight across the feather as possible.* The finer this penciling and *the more numerous the bars, the better.* This penciling should extend from the throat to the very tip of the tail. A well-penciled tail is very desirable, and quite difficult to obtain, as there is a special tendency in the long feathers to lose the straightness across of the markings. Tails penciled squarely across to the very tip can be and are bred, but they are never common. One of the greatest faults to which the plumage is liable is the irregular and "horse-shoe" style of markings which we so often see in the breast, and, in fact, nearly every part of the hen's plumage. This is a most serious defect, and not less to be noticed because of its frequency. A very usual fault is a light breast, or not only light, but covered only with these horse-shoe markings. The birds best marked on the breast are frequently liable to be spotted on the hackle, and this latter fault is certainly much to be preferred to a bad breast. However, the best marking on the breast is never quite equal to that on other parts of the body.

A very desirable point is to have the rows of penciling on one feather fall onto the rows on the next, giving the bird a ruled or lined appearance. A coarsely penciled bird is not to be thought of in these days—although such birds were formerly the rule—as they have a spotty or speckled appearance, which is not the correct thing at all. A finely-penciled wing in hens is almost impossible to find, many of our best show birds being very bad in this respect, the markings being very light and indistinct.

The penciling is much better the first year—or in pullets; with age it becomes cloudy, mossy, or indistinct, so that a well-penciled hen is quite rare. When they do moult out well the second or third season, they are especially valuable, and should be retained for breeding as long as they will breed. All tendency to brownish or chestnut colored feathers (which sometimes make their appearance, although rarely,) should be carefully guarded against, and when they do appear the bird should at once be discarded for breeding purposes.

We have enumerated the faults to which this breed is liable so minutely, not because they are greater than those of many other varieties, but because they require the most skillful breeding to eradicate. As they are among the most beautiful fowls we have, so are they among the most difficult to breed to perfection, and they offer a fine field to intelligent breeders, who like to feel that they owe the perfection of their birds to their own efforts. Those men who want their birds *made for them*, so that they will *breed easily themselves*, had better let them alone, for they should only belong to the intelligent and hard-working fancier, who will find them very pliable, and who *can* reap the reward of his industry and perseverance in beholding in time a fowl that in beauty and utility shall stand unrivaled throughout the world.

Other Points.—The comb in Silver-Penciled Hamburgs is the same as that described in Black Hamburgs, and averages as perfect as in any other variety. It is usually rather smaller, with more "work" or fine points on the top than the comb of the Spangled varieties. The ear-lobe should be pure white, and is usually very good in this respect, it seeming to be one of their firmly-fixed characteristics. The face has the same tendency to white as in the other varieties, and this should be avoided with like caution. In symmetry they are, perhaps, superior to the Spangled varieties, and are equaled only by the Blacks in this respect, birds poor in symmetry being pleasingly scarce. They are not quite so full in the breast as the other varieties we have described, but have an exceedingly graceful carriage, and are upright and sprightly in appearance. Their legs are small, slender, and neat in appearance, and in color, leaden-blue, which should be very dark—approaching black—in young birds.

Points in Breeding Silver-Penciled Hamburgs.—One good point in regard to this variety is that the same birds will breed fine birds of both sexes, if the stock is chosen with judgment. Some breeders use two sets, but we do not consider that they are required, and much prefer to breed from one yard. Of course, as we have said before, there will be, as in all varieties, some strains or families that produce better birds of one sex than the other; still, in this case there should be no great disparity in the quality of the male and female birds. However, as it is possible to breed very good show cockerels from hens with no quality of penciling at all, it is very necessary, in making up a yard for breeding, that the strain of the cock bird should be known to be a well-penciled one. The hens will speak for themselves. It is very satisfactory to remark that our most popular judges favor those cock birds that possess the points most likely to produce good pullets; and if such a bird comes of a strain known to produce good pullets, of a penciling similar in character to those of the hens he is to be put with, it is sufficient. His tail should be black throughout, the sickles black except the clear white edging; the wing-bars should be perceptible, but slight, though the wing-coverts which form it must be darkly penciled on their upper webs. If there be too little color here the pullets will lack color also; if the bar be too dark, the penciling will most likely be coarse, heavy and spotty. As such birds as we have described above are by no means common, and may not be readily procured by the average breeder, we shall also give matings for breeding from two yards, which will be necessary if this is the case; although, be it distinctly understood, the above mating is our choice, and really the only proper one.

For Cockerels.—Mate the best show cockerel you can find with hens much too light in the penciling to be fit for showing—tolerably marked, but markings not heavy enough—and if they are irregular, it is no great matter.

For Pullets.—Mate a very dark cock with the very best hens or pullets you can procure. It will make little difference if the cock's sickles are entirely black, and his body spotted in places; if he is only *dark*, he will throw a fair lot of pullets if the hens be good.

The disadvantage of breeding from these two pens is obvious, as neither strain thus produced can be relied upon to breed in any other way, and many of the pullets hatched, even if they do not show the approach to black spangling already referred to, are apt to have the broad and coarse markings which we are trying to breed out as rapidly as possible.

A cock from the first mating described, if well marked, will throw very fine pullets, while he will reproduce his own likeness in the cockerels.

GOLDEN-PENCILED HAMBURGS.

GOLDEN-PENCILED HAMBURGS.

In point of markings, the Golden are fully as beautiful as the Silver-Penciled Hamburgs, while the golden ground-color, which is their distinguishing feature, while not so popular with the majority of breeders as the silver, may yet be preferred by some. In point of productiveness they equal the Silvers, laying a small, white and finely-flavored egg. The young chicks of both varieties of Penciled Hamburgs are rather delicate; they should not be hatched before April. Another reason in favor of late hatching is that if hatched too early they moult out like old hens at the time they should be laying, and so lose that sharp and rich penciling that is so desirable in pullets.

Plumage.—One of the most important points in the plumage of this variety is the *evenness* of the ground-color, which should be a rich golden-color throughout. Some birds, otherwise good, are very faulty in this respect, the ends of the feathers being a lighter gold than the other parts. These birds, as the season advances, are apt to get still more faded and washed-out in appearance; and, indeed, most birds fade in color from the effects of the sun.

Some hens of a good rich color retain this much better than others, which is a great point in their favor.

In cocks the same fault is common, appearing in the shape of a lighter shade on the ends or tips of the feathers, on the breast and underneath the body; avoid this as far as possible—the more uniform the color, the better.

The penciling should be exactly the same as in the preceding variety, as distinct, and yet as fine as possible, and the more bars across the feather the better—

always providing they are straight across, and clearly defined. The neck-hackle, as in the Silvers, should be clear. The cock is of a darker tint, being almost chestnut in color; he must not, however, be too red or too pale, but very rich in color. The proper tail-feathers are black, the sickles and tail-coverts, or "hangers," a rich black, edged with brown or bronze, very narrow, and clearly defined. The *American Standard of Excellence* gives the required width of this edging as about one-sixteenth of an inch.

Clear black sickles are a great fault, and so is a tail bronzed all over, or with scarcely any black in it, being bronzed all over the sickles. This last kind of a tail is very showy, and used to be a favorite with judges who did not understand Hamburgs, but birds possessing this defect have been proved to produce very poorly penciled pullets.

Other Points.—The comb, ear-lobe, legs and symmetry in the Golden-Penciled Hamburgs should be exactly the same as those described in the Silver-Penciled. In symmetry, especially, they are fully their equal.

The points in breeding are exactly similar to those explained in connection with the preceding variety, and need not be repeated, the best rule being to breed from the very best birds you can find on both sides, care being taken to obtain a rich, even ground-color in all cases.

WHITE HAMBURGS.

WHITE HAMBURGS.

While we undoubtedly owe the White Hamburg to skillful English breeding, it is a variety bred much more generally in America than it is across the water, where it is regarded as a mere sub-variety of Hamburgs. The variety was originally bred in England as an experiment, and was obtained by selecting the lightest Silver-Spangled Hamburgs, both male and female, and mating them together, each year selecting the lightest progeny, until the pure white bird was procured. Thus it will be seen that in spite of all arguments to the contrary, the White Hamburg is really a *pure Hamburg* in every particular. While they were a very pretty variety, they were looked upon with considerable disfavor by the English, who discouraged their breeding, and regarded them as an innovation in the Hamburg family.

It is many years now since they began to be bred in America, and they are much thought of for their many good characteristics, while they figure quite prominently at our principal exhibitions. What has served principally to discourage White Hamburg breeders, is the fact that so many imitations have been made and thrust upon the public under that name, that were really mere mongrels. The *only* true White Hamburgs are those which come from Silver-Spangled or Silver-Penciled Hamburgs, in the manner we have described. Those with White Leghorn or White Dorking crosses are *impositions*, and should be avoided by the fancier, who will readily know them by their clumsy symmetry, large size and coarse combs.

Characteristics of the Variety.—The White Hamburgs should be pure white in plumage throughout, with no signs of that undesirable yellowish tinge so often seen on otherwise good birds. They should be *true Hamburg* in symmetry, avoiding the Leghorn or Dorking build, and they should be (and are) no larger than the other varieties. Size is not a point to be regarded in Hamburgs; it is their laying qualities we look to, and this variety, while not quite up to the others in this respect, is very productive. The comb in White Hamburgs should resemble that described under the heading of Black Hamburgs. They should have a small, round, white ear-lobe, by no means pendent, and bright red face; carriage upright, sprightly and graceful.

The Leg Controversy.—We have so far said nothing concerning the color of legs in White Hamburgs, for the reason that there has been a spirited controversy for many years among breeders as to whether they should be *blue* or *white*. It has been a great nuisance to the American Poultry Association, who have found themselves persuaded, because of specious arguments on both sides, to change their *Standard* at least four times on legs of White Hamburgs. It was originally decided by the *Standard* committee that a white leg was proper. It was afterward changed from white to blue, from blue back to white, then again to blue, and in 1879 to white.

Hon. Lewis F. Allen, who is perhaps our largest and most prominent breeder of the White Hamburg, and who has done as much as any other man to push the breed, says in a clever letter, which, however, betrays his chagrin at the vacillating decrees of the *Standard* committee:

"I have been so disgusted with the doings of the *Standard* committee on the points of fowls that I have determined never again to take any part in its discussions, or show a bird in its exhibitions, although I still keep and breed the White Hamburg with *white legs and beak*, which marks truly belong to them, as they did when I first knew them, in 1870.

"I obtained my original birds from a gentleman who bought them in New York—descendants from imported stock, I was informed. They were then, and still are, *true* Hamburgs in style and form, non-sitters, and nearly constant layers; hardy in temperament, and, in short, very satisfactory birds. They were successfully shown in several of our poultry shows in Buffalo, and won prizes, the white legs and beaks being entirely satisfactory to judges and the society.

"But when the American Poultry Association undertook to make a *Standard* of points for the various varieties of fowls, some of the pretended 'professionals' introduced various innovations, and among them accorded the *blue* leg and beak to the White Hamburg, which was adopted. Consequently, at the next show at Buffalo, my birds were ruled out under the new *blue-leg* regulation. The *Standard* committee had a full meeting during the show, and I went before them and showed the absurdity of the new rule, and the committee decided to reverse the late action and return the points of *white* legs to the White Hamburgs. It has since, however, been changed several times."

Mr. Allen seems to have no doubt but that the *white* leg is entirely proper, and he shows himself to feel injured by the constant changes made in the *Standard*; and indeed it has greatly injured the variety, simply because breeders never could tell how to breed their birds so that they would not be disqualified at the next season's shows. That the point between the two colors is a fine one is proved by the indecision of the *Standard* committee.

. Through all the changes the Rev. C. W. Bolton has stood as firmly by the blue legs as Mr. Allen has by the white ones, and his faith in their propriety has never wavered. Mr. Bolton is one of our most prominent Hamburg men, and has proved his skill as a breeder in showing some excellent stock of the several varieties. He writes us:

"I know perfectly well that my White Hamburgs are *pure* Hamburgs in every respect. I have bred them myself from the Silver-Penciled Hamburgs, with *blue* legs, and all the characteristics of their predecessors. For ten years I have never had a chick with legs of any other color than blue, which shows that the *blue* leg is a firmly fixed characteristic, and properly belongs there."

Why should other varieties of Hamburgs have a blue leg and the White Hamburg a white leg? The blue leg is a distinct Hamburg characteristic.

We believe that when our final and unalterable *Standard* is made, the White Hamburgs will be credited with *blue* legs.

Points in Breeding.—The rule in mating White Hamburgs should be simply to procure the birds which possess the finest combs, ear-lobes and face, pure white plumage and blue legs. Guard against heavy, blocky forms and coarse combs, and pay less attention to size than to proper symmetry.

CARE OF YOUNG CHICKS.

As so few breeders seem to have any clearly-defined ideas as to the proper mode of caring for newly-hatched or growing chicks, and beginners are not only wholly at sea in this respect, but have no place to which they may turn and acquire the information that they have not yet been able to gain through experience (which is by odds the best teacher, as we are seldom able to profit by the experience of others), we have thought best to prepare a few distinct and common-sense instructions, which we have endeavored to render as full and explicit as possible, without being so tedious or complicated as to mislead in any way the novice.

To start with, there is one essential point in raising these delicate little creatures—*care*. Give them plenty of care, and they will thrive—*proper* care, we mean. There are three primary things to be guarded against in caring for very young chickens:

    1. Chilling.
    2. Vermin.
    3. Indigestible food.

For the first week, perhaps, nearly every old hen is faithful to her little brood, and guards them with that maternal tenderness for which she has been made the symbol of motherly love. But this care soon wearies her, and in a few days she begins to neglect them, marching around in the chill and drenching rains of spring, and dragging her little brood after her through the damp grass, entirely oblivious of their sufferings; and one by one they drop off and are left behind, chilled through, or seized with cramp. Only the most persevering are able to keep up, until, perhaps seized with a pang of remorse, she spreads her wings and allows the little ones to find a temporary shelter beneath her warm feathers. Even the strongest often succumb to rheumatism and die after this dangerous exposure. This picture is not overdrawn; it is of common occurrence. A proper coop, therefore, for the hen and chicks, as soon as they are able to leave the nest is, and always will be, regarded as a necessity.

Vermin is the second evil to be guarded against. Examine the chicks carefully when first hatched, and should you find any lice on either them or the hen, let your first move be to rid them of these pests, which will else surely prove fatal to the young birds. Procure some Dalmatian or Persian Insect Powder, and dust them thoroughly with it until their tormentors are exterminated. And here let us recommend *cleanliness* in everything. The tender chicks cannot live in filth, which breeds disease more rapidly than anything else. Keep your coops clean, your houses clean, and your runs clean. It is a very important element of success—indispensable, in fact.

On the *food* depends in a great measure the growth and health of the chicks. *Indigestible* food avoid by all means. By indigestible we mean sloppy and dirty food, and that which is sour. The best feed at first is pure, sweet bread and milk, and hard-boiled eggs and bread crumbs mixed together and crumbled with the fingers. Let them always have access to plenty of pure water. Any form of grain is good for them as soon as they will eat it, and after they are a few days old they will thrive on cracked corn and oatmeal. As they get older whole wheat is an excellent growing food. Green stuff they should have constantly after they are a week old, and if it is too early in the season to give them grass, feed a little lettuce, clipped fine with scissors, at least once a day. At ten days of age they are ready to thrive on whole wheat as they will on nothing else. Give them plenty of bone now, and never let your efforts flag to *keep them growing*. When the chicks are fully feathered the many dangers which constantly beset the lives of the youngsters are usually safely passed, and, barring all accidents, it is pretty safe to suppose that they will now pull through.

Nine out of every ten breeders then breathe a sigh of relief, and settle down to a quiet summer, or leave home. The tenth breeder is sharper. He not only stays at home, but he redoubles his attentions to his young flock. He realizes that *now* is the time when these future prize winners demand all the care which he can bestow to *keep them growing* finely. And he is right. It won't do to slack up now. They need a different kind of care. From endeavoring to keep the breath of life in the little things, he changes his attention to a system of judicious feeding, calculated to keep them growing rapidly during the propitious summer weather. Alas, for the chick whom the cold weather catches half-developed and half-feathered! August, September and October are the finest growing months in the year, and those chicks which now have a good start, if properly cared for and judiciously forced, will be the ones to make a fine showing at the next winter's exhibitions. In growing they need plenty of bone meal and oyster shells, and an occasional supply of fresh meat, if worms are not plentiful. Do not force them too much, as in Hamburgs it induces the comb to lop and grow to an undesirable size. Again let us recommend plenty of pure, cool water, and vegetable food in quantity. Little attentions are never thrown away, but will be amply repaid in time in a vigorous, large and healthy flock of fowls.

PREPARING HAMBURGS FOR EXHIBITION.

Condition means everything in showing Hamburgs, and without it many a fine bird comes home from a show minus a prize that could easily have been won had its owner known how to properly fit it for exhibition. By "fitting it" we do not refer to the unscrupulous tricks resorted to by unprincipled scoundrels who *mutilate* and torture their birds to bring them within the requirements of the *Standard*, but to the legitimate preparation to which it is not only allowable to subject a bird, but without which it is really a pity to send a good bird to the show room. We are not going to recommend any practices which may not be fully known and approved of by any judge, so that any exhibitor may have no hesitation in following our instructions. For at least three weeks before the exhibition all varieties of Hamburgs should be confined in a darkened coop—not too dark, but with just light enough to enable them to see to eat. We recommend this for the following reasons:

1. It serves to whiten in an astonishing degree the ear-lobe. We have often seen a bird which, when placed in the darkened coop, had ear-lobes discolored by exposure to the weather, come out at the end of three weeks with pure milky-white ear-lobes *throughout*. During this confinement the ear-lobes should be washed

each day with sweet milk, applied with a sponge.

2. This confinement is of great value in promoting a rich luster to the plumage, making each color stand out distinctly, and giving the feathers that glossy appearance so much desired. This matter of plumage is one of primary importance. In Black Hamburgs the greenish gloss should be brought out as much as possible, and in order to do this confinement in darkened quarters is necessary. After they (the Blacks we are now referring to) have been confined until about a week previous to the show, they should be taken from the coop, and their feathers rubbed down daily with a piece of flannel cloth. Hold the bird firmly on your lap, and pass the cloth lightly down the back from the neck to the tip of the tail, and keep up this rubbing steadily for the required time, say fifteen minutes. You will be surprised to see the magnificent gloss brought out upon birds that before were even slightly dull in appearance of plumage. If your birds have the undesirable purple tinge, this will bring it out more than you would wish, but if they have the *greenish* sheen, it will make them glisten in a manner to delight your eyes.

The Whites are much improved likewise by this confinement, as it gives the plumage a clear milky-white color, and it loses under this treatment the yellowish cast they have acquired by exposure to the weather; only, if they are bad in this respect, they should be put in their darkened quarters at least a month previous to the exhibition. With Golden-Penciled and Spangled Hamburgs this darkened coop is of much assistance in bringing out the greenish spangles and brightening and enriching the ground-color; and with these varieties, as with the Blacks, we would recommend the gentle rubbing with coarse flannel.

Silver-Spangled and Penciled birds gain by their darkened quarters a clear and distinct appearance in their markings, as it makes the ground-color a beautiful white, furnishing a desirable background for the colored feathers.

There is no help for a bad comb or a white face. The best way is never to allow a bird with these defects to see the inside of a show room. Birds with a tendency to scaly legs should have them rubbed with Stoddard's Poultry Ointment, beginning at least two weeks before the show. If breeders would only attend to this repulsive appearance of the legs in time, or whenever it makes its appearance, and treat it as above, these remarks would be unnecessary. It is an eye-sore in any bird, but particularly disgusting on the neat, slender legs of the Hamburgs.

In fitting birds for show they should have a wholesome variety of food, wheat and buckwheat being the staples. A little sunflower seed, fed at judicious intervals for the six weeks previous to the show, has a very desirable effect in giving them the gloss and finish so desirable, and which is always observed in prize birds.

When the time arrives to coop the birds and start them off for the show, great care should be taken that they are in proper trim. As each bird is cooped it should be carefully examined to see that there are no symptoms of disease, or any foul feathers in the plumage. Then take a sponge and carefully wash the comb, wattles, face and legs with a mixture of equal parts of sweet oil and alcohol, applying as little as is possible to procure the desired effect — which is, by the way, a remarkable brightening of the comb, wattles and face, giving them a rich, healthy and bright appearance, and imparting to the legs a beautiful gloss, which brings out their color with good effect.

If these instructions are carefully followed, you will hardly recognize in the smart, clean-looking bird that graces the exhibition coop, the soiled and dull appearing fowl you began fitting three weeks before. It may require a certain amount of time to attend to these details properly, but will you not feel amply repaid by beholding the prize card on your coop, and having your brother fanciers comment upon the fine condition of your birds?

HINTS TO JUDGES.

Very few of the leading and popular judges at our exhibitions are Hamburg *breeders*, and realizing this, it should not be difficult to imagine the chagrin and disappointment of an *experienced* breeder of these varieties when he stands by at a show and sees the judge award the premiums to birds with many and glaring faults, to his eyes, but which are never noticed by this oracle of the show room, who makes his figures with a business-like alacrity, strongly savoring of ignorance to the close observer, and appears thoroughly satisfied that he is "up to snuff," when in reality he has been absurdly unjust in his awards.

There is no breed which needs so careful examination from the judge as the Hamburg, in each variety, not only on account of the many points to be considered, but because there is *no* breed so subject to the manipulations of unprincipled exhibitors, or where there is more lynx-eyed vigilance required from the judge to guard him against the impositions of those pests of the show room — *trimmers*.

The points to which a judge should devote his attention in judging Hamburgs may be divided into four divisions, namely: 1, head; 2, plumage; 3, symmetry; 4, condition. Beginning with the first of these, we find included under this topic — comb, wattles, ear-lobes and face. There is no point in which Hamburgs are subject to such extensive manipulation as in the comb, and some of the practices which have been detected are of the most cruel nature. Cases where needles and pins have been inserted lengthwise of the comb to keep it from lapping while the judge is making his rounds, have been of common occurrence, although we are pleased to note that as more good and small-sized combs are being bred yearly, this practice seems to be falling into disuse. These instruments of torture are usually inserted just before the judges examine the birds, and withdrawn by means of pinchers immediately after the awards have been made, so that they are really difficult to discover. Where these needles are left in the comb, the most intense suffering ensues, and Mr. Hewitt has drawn a most harrowing picture of the tortures the poor bird is obliged to undergo. He says: "On the second day, the comb becomes most intolerably inflamed, and I have seen a fowl in its agony bend the head down, raise its foot, as with the intention of relieving the comb by scratching it, stop the movement midway without touching the comb at all, and then tremble like an aspen-leaf." When cases of such barbarity are detected, the exhibitor should be remorselessly drummed out of the exhibition and the fraternity. A very common fault in combs is a hollow or depression in the center; and this is usually treated by cutting a wedge-shaped piece out of the middle, and stitching the outside portions tightly till joined and healed. Stitches put in for one purpose or other are often found, and, we regret to add, are employed far oftener than found. Small irregularities in shape and points are simply shaved off. Such mutilations are quickly discerned by a practiced eye in the smooth appearance of the comb when it has been cut, but as frequently this appearance is due to a past accident, judges should not act hastily upon suspicion.

Particular attention should be paid to the "work" or fine points of the comb; the more numerous they are, the better. Hollows in the front of the comb, above the beak, are common and objectionable, and should be severely cut. Pullets should have *small* and well-shaped combs. We recommend cutting large combs in pullets, as they are almost certain to fall over with age.

The face is also subject to painting red when it has a tendency to white, and this is often discovered by the difference in the shade of the comb and face, although sometimes the similarity of color is so perfect as to defy detection. When we suspect painting, a gentle rubbing usually suffices to prove if our suspicions are correct. This white in the face is a direct disqualification in Black Hamburgs according to the American *Standard*, but as we seldom find a two or three year old cock without it, we think the *Standard* should not thus *disqualify* old birds, but "cut severely as a defect." Cockerels with this white face should be thrown out without remorse.

Ear-lobes are often painted white, and sometimes quite cleverly, but this is usually so bungling an operation as to be readily detected, if you examine it carefully. Ear-lobes should be round and small. Cut large, irregularly-shaped, and above all, *pendent* ear-lobes. The bluish tinge often seen on Hamburg ear-lobes should not be cut except in cases of comparison. We do not like it, but it is often occasioned by confinement, and is not a direct blemish. Wattles should be small and well rounded. We recommend cutting a pendent wattle, such as is proper to the Leghorn varieties.

Our second division treats of plumage, and here again the trimmer finds a broad field of labor. White feathers in Blacks are pulled out, but as these usually appear in the wings, if at all, the absence of flight feathers should be accepted as proof of the previous existence of white feathers. If there is any tendency at all to white in this variety, it will usually be found by holding the bird by the legs head downward, when the fluff feathers under the tail and between the legs will be found to possess small white tips. We found the first prize birds at a recent show distinctly tipped with white here, but the judge had never noticed it. In the case of the spangled varieties, large quantities of feathers are often extracted from the breast and back, when they are so numerous that the black spangles run together.

This trimming out process, which is, of course, done to show the color between the spangles, is very difficult of detection, and almost impossible to positively prove. In the penciled varieties the attention of the trimmer is turned to the tail of the cocks. A finely-penciled tail is a rarity, and when a fine set of well-marked sickles are obtained they are sometimes preserved "for future reference" (as it were), and often figure in several different birds before they are worn out. As these well-marked sickles often grow on a bird with a poor comb, the owner usually selects his best marked bird otherwise, extracts the poor sickles, and inserts the good ones in their place. The fastening may get loose during the show, and then drop out, exposing the fraud at once. These false sickles, however, are usually dull in color, lacking the gloss of healthy feathers, and can be usually detected by a judge who has his wits about him and is on the alert. Still, they are sometimes so cleverly doctored as to defy discovery, unless subjected to such harsh treatment as few judges feel justified in using upon mere suspicion. A dark, glossy, sharply-edged tail on a cock with very slight wing-bars should always excite suspicion.

Another frequent practice is dyeing feathers. This is often detected by the absence of the glossy appearance seen on the remainder of the plumage. Frequently, however, off-colored feathers will be plucked out, skillfully colored and glossed, and successfully reinstated in their places, with little chance of their being discovered. In spangled and penciled birds, imperfect markings or blotches are often bleached out with acids, and proper markings given the feathers with grease-paints, which assimilate with the oily substance in the feather, and render detection almost impossible. These various frauds make the task of a conscientious Hamburg judge one of unusual anxiety and responsibility. We may be blamed for mentioning these vile practices, but we believe that any evil that may arise from our furnishing hints to the unscrupulous will be more than counterbalanced by putting judges on their guard who are much too apt to pass over these points rapidly and carelessly.

The third division treats of symmetry, and right here let us say that there is no point in judging Hamburgs so much neglected as this most important one. We were dismayed to hear a judge, who was examining birds recently, say: "You are pretty safe to cut a Hamburg one point for symmetry." What did he mean? Simply, we suppose, that he knew so little about this quality that he resolved to cover his ignorance by refusing to admit any bird to be perfect in this respect. There are too many judges, alas, who agree with him, because they know not what symmetry means. We have described the symmetry of Hamburgs under the heading of the Black variety, and so need not repeat it. Only let us again warn judges to discriminate between the undesirable *Game* shape, and the equally improper *Dorking* mould in judging these birds. The Hamburg symmetry is peculiar to the breed, and cannot be mistaken, and as fully one-half the birds exhibited incline either to the Game or Dorking symmetry, the distinct difference in shape should be understood by every judge, and severely cut if not correct.

Our last division refers to condition, and this, also, is of much importance in judging Hamburgs. It counts from five to ten points in making up a perfect bird, and we believe there is not one case out of ten where dark or dusty plumage, discolored comb or soiled legs are cut by the judge. Unless the bird has decided symptoms of roup, or other disease, it is simply passed over. A good judge invariably makes the point of condition a primary one. It means a fresh, well-kept condition of the comb and head, a fine, glossy plumage, upright and active appearance, and clean, shining legs.

There is an indescribable difference between a healthy, active, well-bred bird and one that, although it may be descended from pure stock, having correct markings and the like, yet lacks vivacity, spirit and a general air of *aristocracy*. If there be one breed of fowls above others more worthy of being called the "upper-crust of poultry-dom," we are inclined to the opinion the breed under our consideration is that one.

Now, every man is not fitted to become a good judge of poultry, even if he go through the regular process, any more than every one can become an exact musician by undergoing the necessary course of training. There is an inborn something that distinguishes one person from another and certain it is that ideas of form, grace and coloring, above the ordinary, are to be found in the composition of our best judges.

The question is often asked by officers of agricultural and horticultural fairs, as well as by those of poultry exhibitions, if it is not possible to have awards made without producing the hard feelings and unsatisfactory results generally following. And we answer, "No!"—as long as no more pains are taken in the selection of judges on the score of their particular fitness for the position they are called upon to fill. On their efficiency turn the questions of success, harmony, and the keeping and securing of the public confidence and patronage.

We hope we have not been too severe upon judges in this chapter. A really good judge will see the force of our arguments, and in the case of the indifferent ones, we trust *verbum sapientibus omnes est*.

Lector House believes that a society develops through a two-fold approach of continuous learning and adaptation, which is derived from the study of classic literary works spread across the historic timeline of literature records. Therefore, we aim at reviving, repairing and redeveloping all those inaccessible or damaged but historically as well as culturally important literature across subjects so that the future generations may have an opportunity to study and learn from past works to embark upon a journey of creating a better future.

This book is a result of an effort made by Lector House towards making a contribution to the preservation and repair of original ancient works which might hold historical significance to the approach of continuous learning across subjects.

HAPPY READING & LEARNING!

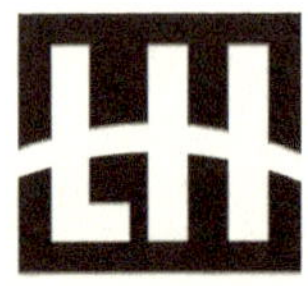

LECTOR HOUSE LLP
E-MAIL: lectorpublishing@gmail.com